Let's DRAW!

CATS

How2DrawAnimals

Brimming with creative inspiration, how-to projects, and useful information to enrich your everyday life, quarto.com is a favorite destination for those pursuing their interests and passions.

First published in 2022 by Walter Foster Jr., an imprint of The Quarto Group.
100 Cummings Center, Suite 265D, Beverly, MA 01915, USA.
T (978) 282-9590 F (978) 283-2742 www.quarto.com • www.walterfoster.com

Walter Foster Jr. titles are also available at discount for retail, wholesale, promotional, and bulk purchase. For details, contact the Special Sales Manager by email at specialsales@quarto.com or by mail at The Quarto Group, Attn: Special Sales Manager, 100 Cummings Center, Suite 265D, Beverly, MA 01915, USA.

ISBN: 978-0-7603-8070-3

Digital edition published in 2022
eISBN: 978-0-7603-8071-0

10 9 8 7 6 5 4 3 2

TABLE OF CONTENTS

TOOLS & MATERIALS

Welcome! You don't need much to start learning how to draw. Anyone can draw with just a pencil and piece of scrap paper, but if you want to get more serious about your art, additional artist's supplies are available.

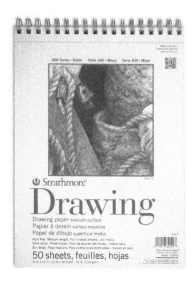

PAPER If you choose printer paper, buy a premium paper that is thick enough and bright. Portable sketch pads keep all your drawings in one place, which is convenient. For more detailed art pieces, use a fine art paper.

PENCILS Standard No. 2 pencils and mechanical pencils are great to start with and inexpensive. Pencils with different graphite grades can be very helpful when shading because a specific grade (such as 4H, 2B, or HB) will only get so dark.

PENCIL SHARPENER Electric sharpeners are faster than manual ones, but they also wear down pencils faster. It's most economical to use an automatic one for inexpensive pencils and a manual sharpener for expensive ones.

ERASERS Some erasers can smear, bend, and even tear your paper, so get a good one that erases cleanly without smudges. Kneaded erasers are pliable and can be molded for precise erasing. They leave no residue, and they last a long time.

PENS If you want to outline a drawing after sketching it, you can use a regular Sharpie® pen or marker. For more intricate pieces, try Micron® pens, which come in a variety of tip thicknesses.

DRAWING BASICS

How to Draw Shapes

For the first steps of each project in this book, you will be drawing basic shapes as guide lines. Use light, smooth strokes and don't press down too hard with your pencil. If you sketch lightly at first, it will be easier to erase if you make a mistake.

You'll be drawing a lot of circles, which many beginning artists find difficult to create. These circles do not have to be perfect because they are just guides, but if you want to practice making better circles, try the four-marks method, as shown below.

1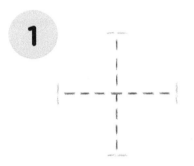

Mark where you want the top of the circle and, directly below, make another mark for the bottom. Do the same for the sides of the circle. If it helps, lightly draw a dotted line to help you place the other mark.

2

Once you have the four marks spaced apart equally, connect them using curved lines.

3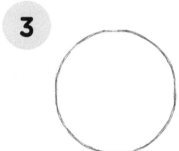

Erase any dotted lines you created, and you have a circle!

ADDITIONAL SHAPES While circles are usually what people find the most challenging, there are many other lines and shapes that you should practice and master. An arc can become a muzzle or tongue. Triangles can be ears, teeth, or claws. A football shape can become an eye. A curvy line can make a tail and an angled line a leg. Study the animal and note the shapes that stand out to you.

How to Shade

The final step to drawing an animal is to add shading so that it looks three-dimensional, and then adding texture so that it looks furry, feathery, smooth, or scaly. To introduce yourself to shading, follow the steps below.

1

Understand your pencil with a value scale. Using any pencil, start to shade lightly on one side and gradually darken your strokes toward the other side. This value scale will show you how light and dark your pencil can be.

2

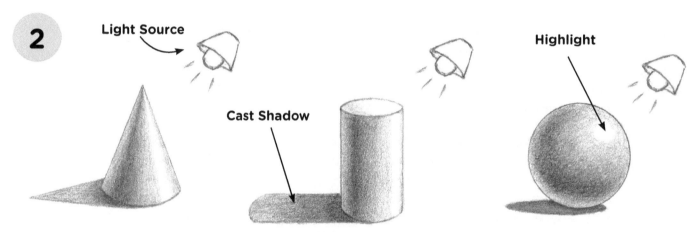

Light Source

Cast Shadow

Highlight

Apply the value scale to simple shapes. Draw simple shapes and shade them to make them look three-dimensional. Observe shadows in real life. Study how the light interacts with simple objects and creates shadows. Then try drawing what you see.

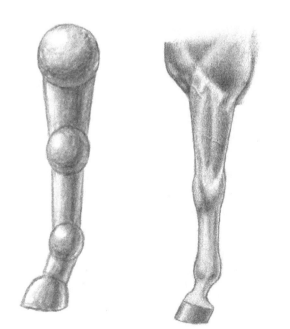

3

Practice with more complex objects. Once you're comfortable shading simple objects, move on to more complex ones. Note, for example, how a horse's leg is made up of cylinders and spheres. Breaking down your subject into simple shapes makes it easier to visualize the shadows.

How to Add Texture

Take what you've learned about shading one step further by adding texture to your drawings.

FURRY

One quick pencil stroke creates a single hair. Keep adding more quick, short strokes and you'll get a furry texture. Separate each individual stroke a bit so that the white of the paper comes through.

Create stripes and patterns by varying the pressure on your pencil to get different degrees of tonal value.

Make sure that your strokes follow the forms of the animal. As you shade a furry animal, use strokes that go in the general direction of the fur growth. The fur here follows the form of a simple sphere.

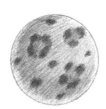

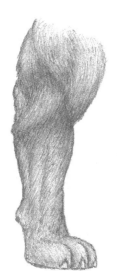

This is how to add fur to a complex form, which is easier if you know the animal's anatomy. In order to show the muscle structure, this image shows an exaggerated example of a lion's front leg and paw.

SMOOTH

For very short fur or smooth skin, add graphite evenly. Blend with a cotton swab, blending stump, or piece of tissue if needed.

SCALY

For scaly animals like reptiles or dragons, create each individual scale with a tiny arc. Then add shadows to make the form look three-dimensional.

For a much easier way to get a scaly look, just add a bunch of squiggles! Make the squiggles darker in areas of pattern, as well as when adding shadows.

FEATHERED When adding texture to feathered animals, approach it as you would with fur or with smooth skin. Use a series of short strokes for fine or fluffy feathers. For smooth feathers, use even, blended value.

CAT HEAD DETAIL

1

Lightly draw a big circle as a guide for the cat's head. Then add two guide lines inside the circle, which will help you place the facial features later. In these first few steps, remember to sketch lightly at first so that it's easy to erase if you make a mistake.

2

Draw basic shapes for guides to add in the eyes, muzzle, and ears later on.

3

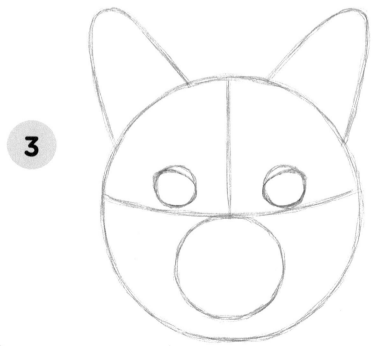

Now begin on the eyes. Make the top, outer edges of the eyes thicker for the eyelashes. Whatever you do to one side, you should do to the other side to keep the cat's symmetry.

4

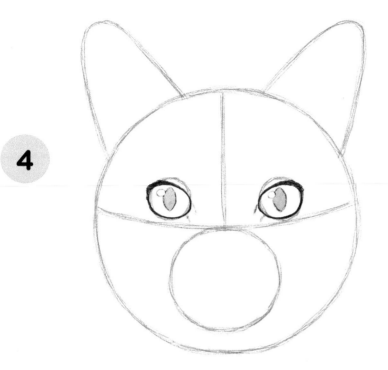

In the middle of each eye, sketch a thin, long oval for the cat's pupils. Off to the side of each pupil, draw a tiny circle for a highlight. Shade the pupils, but don't overlap the inside of the highlight circles. Then add a couple of short lines on the inner, lower edges of the eyes to extend the corners of the eyes.

5

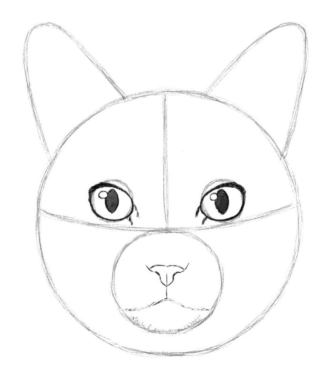

Lightly sketch the nose as a small triangle. Darken the edges using wavy lines and draw a short, vertical line at the bottom. Then add the mouth and chin under the nose with a series of short strokes to represent the fur.

6

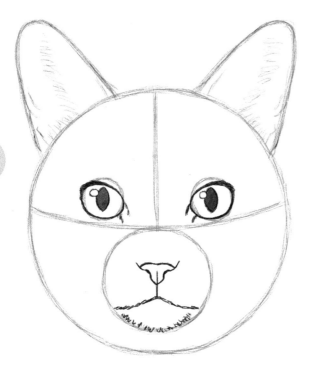

Darken the arcs on the head for the ears. Draw a few short, curved lines inside the shape, near the bottom, to give the ears more structure. Then add a series of strokes across the middle of the shape for the fur found inside the ears. Make the ears look as similar as you can.

7

As you draw the sides of the head, follow the path of the original circle but make the shape a bit wider and curve the line inside the circle toward the chin.

8

Draw a series of short strokes within the shape of the head to show the cat's facial structure and fur. Add some strokes along the lower edge of the main circle for a bit of the neck.

9

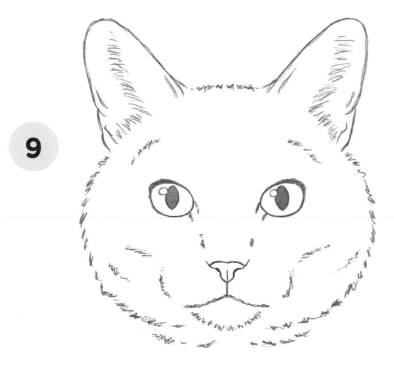

For a cleaner look, erase as much as you can of the initial guide lines. Then re-draw any final sketch lines you may have accidentally erased.

10

Study the image carefully, noting the areas of light and dark. See where the stripes are on the pattern and how most of your pencil strokes will be short and quick for the fur. Some areas will have longer, lighter strokes, such as in the ears; other areas will have smooth shading, such as in the eyes and on the nose. Add a few small, dark spots on the outer edges of the muzzle for the base of the cat's whiskers. Finally, add some value to the lower part of the head to create shadows.

SHADING Remember that shading can take a very long time to complete, so be patient and take breaks. Slowly build up the value by adding more and more strokes until you're happy with the result, and make sure to use pencil strokes that go in the general direction of the fur. It also requires a lot of practice to be able to shade well, so you may want to make a copy of your final sketch so you can try several times.

CAT SLEEPING

1

Draw a circle on the left side as a guide for the head. Add guide lines inside the head circle to help you add facial features later. Then draw another circle on the right as a guide for the cat's backside.

2

Finish up your guide lines in this step, adding a small circle for the muzzle, triangles for ears, and a big, rounded shape for the body.

3

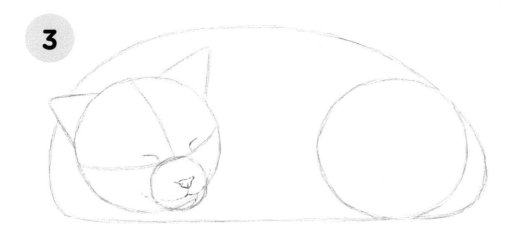

Draw the cat's closed eyes inside the head as small, angled lines. Sketch the triangular nose, and once you are happy with the shape, darken the lines. Then, under the nose, draw curved lines with short strokes for the mouth. Finally, add the chin and the lower jaw.

4

Under the head on the left side, draw the first paw, which is made up of curved lines.

5

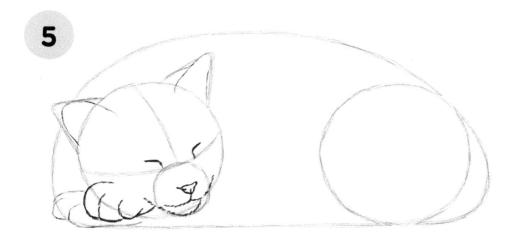

After drawing the other paw, move on to the outer ears. This step also consists of straight and curved lines.

6

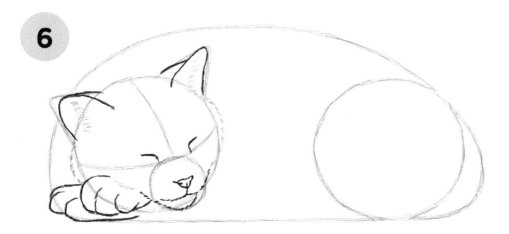

Use a series of strokes inside the ears and along the shape of the cat's face. These short strokes create a fur-like texture.

7

Using the bottom edge of the initial body shape as a guide, draw the tail. Follow the path of the guide and draw a series of strokes along it to make it look furry. Curve the lines upward on the right side so that the tail connects to the cat's body.

8

Use the big, initial shape as a guide to draw the rest of the body. To the right of the head, draw a couple of long lines made up of short strokes for the top parts of the cat's legs.

9

For a cleaner look, erase as much as you can of the initial guide lines, and then clean up your sketch. Stop here for an all-white cat or move on to the final step to shade in your drawing.

10

When shading, vary the pressure on your pencil to get different degrees of tonal value. Note the light values around the eyes, mouth, paws, and ears; the medium value at the edges of the ears, in the head, and in the lighter areas of the pattern; and dark values in the striped pattern. Finally, add a cast shadow underneath the body so your cat doesn't appear to be floating.

RAGDOLL

1

Start by drawing a big circle for the Ragdoll's body and another circle for the head. The head circle should be about one-third the size of the body circle. Place the circles close together so that the neck isn't too long. Then add some guide lines in the head and an angled line at the bottom for the leg.

2

Finish up your guide lines with two triangular shapes as guides for the ears, a small circle as a guide for the cat's muzzle, and several more curved lines for the rest of the body.

3

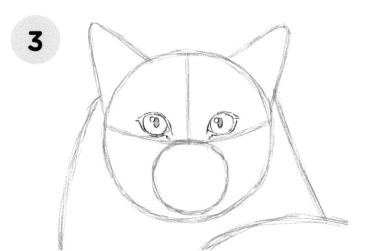

Inside the head, on top of the horizontal construction guide, lightly sketch the eyes. When you get the size and position of all the lines right, darken the shapes. Don't forget to add a tiny circle for a highlight!

4

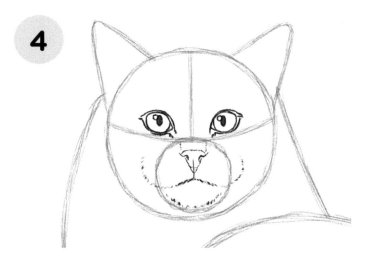

Draw the triangle-like nose, adding all of the extra detail lines and the curved nostrils on the sides. Draw a few short strokes above it for the furry bridge of the nose. Then use short strokes to draw the mouth and chin. Note how wide the muzzle is compared to the other cats in this book.

5

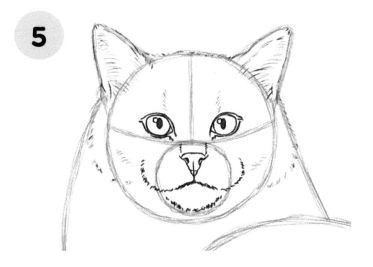

Use the triangular shapes on top of the head as guides to draw the ears. Then add some quick strokes inside for the fur that's inside the ears. Use quick, short strokes to create the head, and add some additional strokes inside the face to further define the head.

6

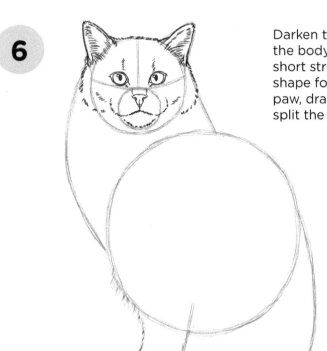

Darken the shapes on the lower, left side of the body to create the first front leg. Use short strokes at the top as you darken the shape for the long fur found there. Inside the paw, draw a couple of short, curved lines to split the toes.

7

On the left side of the front leg, draw a similar shape for the other leg. Then draw a big, curved shape for the fluffy tail. Use short strokes as you draw the shape for a furry texture.

8

Now finish your Ragdoll sketch. Simply darken the outer edges of the guides using short strokes to create the furry shape of the body. Between the tail and the front leg, draw a short, curved shape for the hind paw. Then add a few more short strokes inside the body for detail on the fur.

9

Tidy up your sketch. Erase the guide lines and re-draw any lines you'd like to fix.

STROKE DIRECTION As you shade the body, use strokes that go in the general direction of the fur. The strokes on the head should radiate out from the nose, while the strokes on the body should be mainly vertical.

10

Ragdolls can have a variety of coat patterns, but for this pattern, use a darker value on the head except for the muzzle and the area between the eyes. As you shade, separate each stroke a bit so that the white of the paper comes through and creates a more furry texture. Once you add a darker value on the shadowed areas, you're done!

SIAMESE

Lightly draw three circles, two as guides for the body and one for the head. Leave enough room on the page for the tail and legs. Then add guides inside of the head shape to help you with the facial features later.

Using simple lines and shapes, add the other guide lines for the muzzle, ears, body, tail, and legs. Note how the legs bend where the joints and feet will be.

3

Now lightly sketch the eyes. Note how the eye on the right is a slightly different shape because of the angle of the cat's head. When you get the placement and shapes of the eyes right, darken the lines.

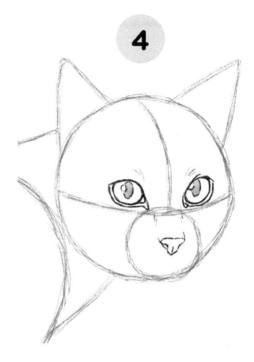

4

Finish the eyes with a dark pupil and highlight, paying close attention to their placement. Then add some short strokes above the eye for the brow and below for the bridge of the nose. Then draw the triangle-like nose and its details.

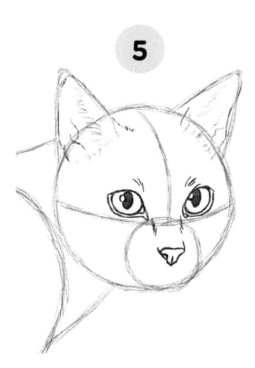

5

Move to the ears, making the tips shorter and rounder than the guides, and extend them inside of the head past the edge of the main circle. Draw a series of quick, short strokes inside the ears for the fur found there. Draw a few curved lines within the shape as well to give the ear internal structure.

6

With quick, short strokes, draw the mouth and chin. Finish the head using the main circle as a guide. When you draw the right side of the head, curve the line in toward the muzzle to make the head leaner.

7

For each leg, follow the basic path of the guide and lightly sketch the shape of the leg around it. The tops of the legs are wider than the bottoms. When you get the shapes right, darken the lines using quick, short strokes to represent the fur. Add curved lines at the tip of the feet to show the toes.

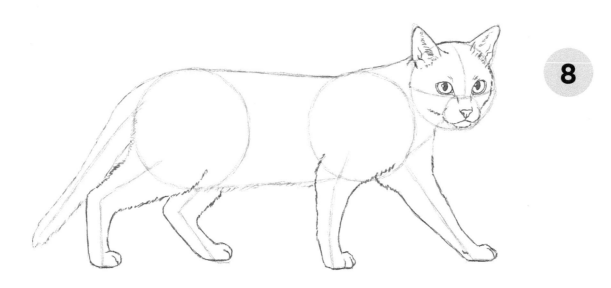

8

Use the remaining lines as guides to draw the rest of the body. Simply darken the outer edges of the initial guides to create the shape of the body. Use quick, short strokes on the left and underside to create shaggy fur. Finish up your cat by drawing the tail.

9

Tidy up your sketch and get ready to shade your drawing to give it the distinct Siamese look.

10

Use a dark value for the outside of the ears, the face, tail, and feet. As you shade, use strokes that go in the general direction of the fur. Use a lighter value as you reach the top and sides of the head and the bottom part of the muzzle. On the legs, the value should be light at the top and gradually get darker. Shade the rest of the body using a light to medium value. Finally, add some shadows to further define the body shape, as well as a cast shadow underneath.

COAT PATTERNS You can use these projects as templates for any cat and shade it how you want. Instead of making this cat a Siamese, try making it an all-black or white cat, or give it any pattern you want! Draw up to step 9 and make copies of your drawing. Then try shading in different patterns to practice.

CAT STRETCHING

Lightly draw three circles. The head will be on the left and the rear will on the right. Note the sizes and placement of these circles.

On the head, draw a curved horizontal line, triangle ears, and a muzzle. Then connect the three circles with slightly curved lines.

2

Finish up your guides by adding the stretched-out front feet, as well as the hind legs and tail.

3

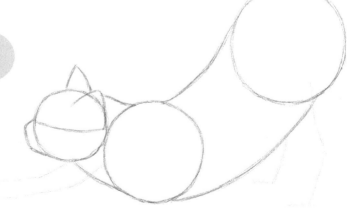

Draw the face, including the closed eyes, nose, mouth, and chin. The eye on the left is barely visible.

5

Use the triangle-like lines on the head as guides to draw the cat's ears. Inside the ear facing the viewer, draw a series of short lines to indicate the structure and fur.

6

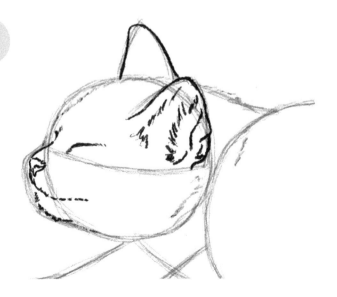

Draw the rest of the head with quick, short strokes along the basic path of the initial circle. Leave a gap along the lower, right side where the head connects to the neck and body.

Use the long horizontal line on the bottom, left side as a guide to draw the cat's first leg. The base or right side of the leg should be thick, and it should gradually get thinner toward the foot. Add a couple of curved lines at the tip for the toes and use quick, short strokes to show the fur.

7

8

Sketch the hind leg lightly at first as you draw around the guide. Use furrier strokes near the top of the leg and add a couple of curved lines at the tip of the foot for the toes.

Draw the visible portions of the legs on the other side of the body using the first legs as guides.

9

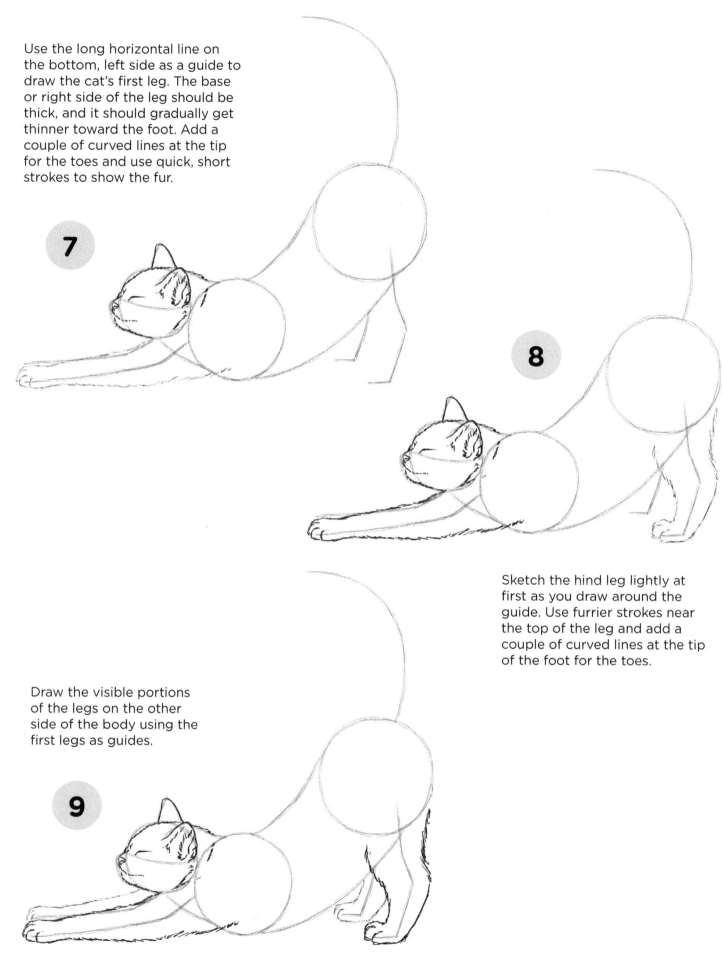

Use the remaining lines and shapes as guides to draw the rest of the body and tail. Add longer strokes on the bottom where there is shaggier fur, and draw some strokes along the back, near the head, to emphasize the skin folds among the fur.

10

Clean up your sketch. Stop here if you'd like an all-white cat.

11

12

Add some shading to your drawing to give it more dimension and volume. Then add a cast shadow underneath so it doesn't appear to be floating. For this cat, use a medium value for the base and add a dark value on top for stripes. Leave the eyes, mouth, and feet white.

KITTEN

1

Lightly sketch three circles as guides for the head and body. Note how the head circle overlaps one of the body circles.

2

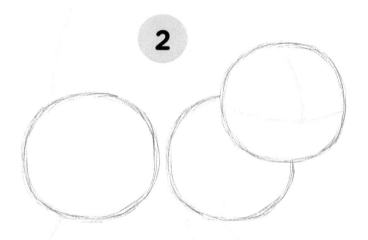

Draw two curved lines inside the head to help you place the facial features later on. Then add three guides for the legs and a line for the tail.

3

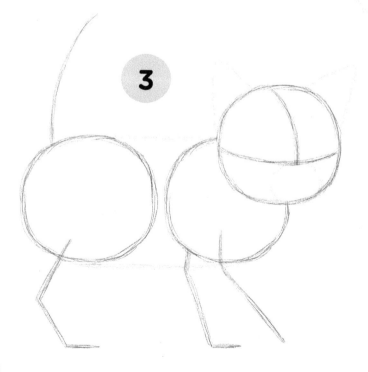

Finish up your guide lines by connecting the body shapes and adding guides for the ears and muzzle.

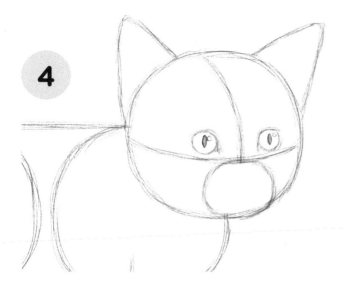

4

Draw the eyes inside the head using the initial lines as guides for placement. Don't forget the two tiny circles to represent highlights in the eyes. Shade the outline of the eyes for extra detail.

WHISKERS Most cats have white whiskers, so they aren't always visible in a drawing. Feel free to add whiskers in white pencil or to leave them off. Take a look at the Maine Coon on page 44 to see how whiskers can be added to your drawings.

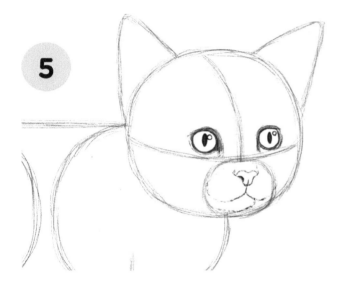

5

Now add the nose, mouth, and chin inside the muzzle circle. Begin the nose by lightly sketching a small triangle. After completing the nose, use quick, short strokes and curving lines to create the mouth.

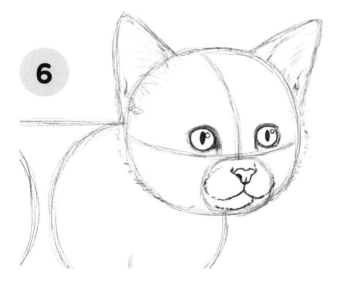

6

Make the ears a bit rounder and draw a few more lines inside for the inner ear structure. Add quick, long strokes for the longer fur inside. Then finish the head by simply following the path of the initial head circle with quick, short strokes for a fuzzy texture.

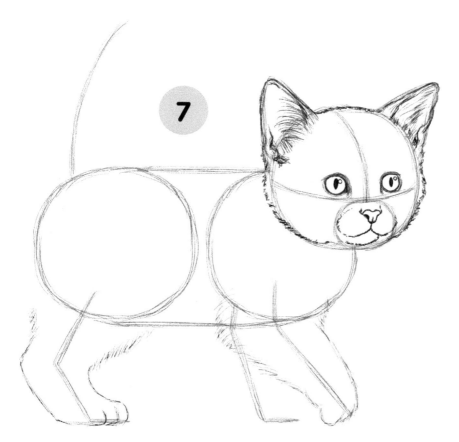

7

In this step, draw two of the kitten's legs, making sure to use quick, short strokes for the furry parts. Add a couple of curved lines on the lifted front leg for the paw and two small lines on the back foot for the toes.

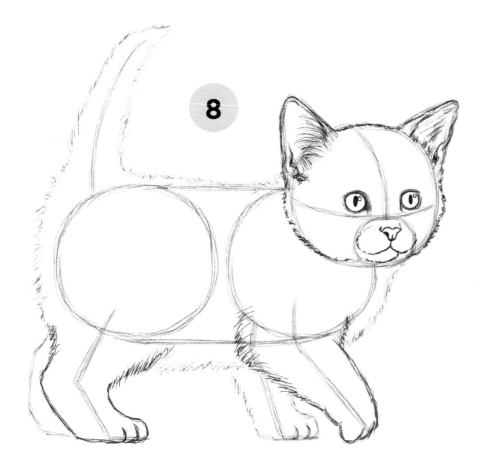

8

Finish up the kitten's body with quick, short strokes. Then draw what's visible of the other two legs. Don't forget a couple of lines on the front paw for the toes.

9

Once you erase your guide lines, you have a completed sketch of a kitten! Stop here if you'd like or move on to the final step to add shading to your drawing.

Give your kitten some dimension and volume with shading. Add the cast shadow underneath so it doesn't appear to be floating. To create this tabby pattern, add a series of short stripes throughout the body by shifting the pressure on your pencil to get different tonal values. You can also add a solid value to the kitten's entire body for a simpler drawing. Make sure to use pencil strokes that go in the same direction that the fur would grow.

10

BENGAL

1

Sketch three circles for the Bengal's head and body. Bengals have small heads in relation to their bodies, so don't draw the head circle too big.

2

Draw several curved construction lines inside the head, and then draw four lines for the legs. Note the angles on the hind legs.

3

After drawing the guides for the ears, muzzle, neck, body, and tail, you have completed your initial sketch and can begin adding the details.

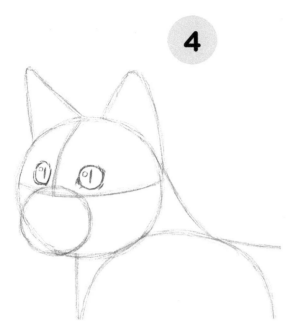

4

Use the initial lines as guides for size and placement of the eyes. The eye on the right should be a bit bigger because of the perspective of the turned head. Add the details, including the highlight circles, slit pupils, and details outside of the eyes.

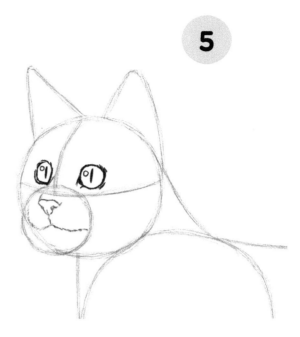

5

Now sketch the nose and top part of the mouth.

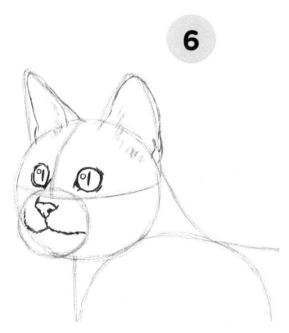

6

Darken the triangle-like shapes on top of the head to create the ears. Add a few curved shapes to give the ear structure and use long strokes inside for the fur found there.

7

Finish the shape of the head with quick, short strokes for a fur-like texture. Draw a curved line made up of short strokes under the mouth for the chin. Bengals have short fur, so don't make these strokes too long.

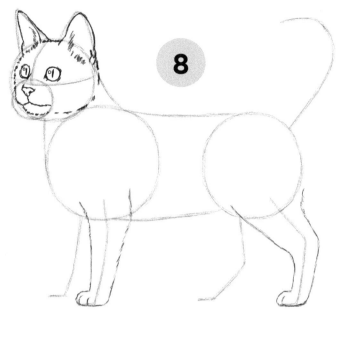

8

Following the leg guides, draw the legs that are on this side of the body. Notice how much wider the top of the hind leg is compared to the front leg, as well as the bend at the joint. Don't forget the toes!

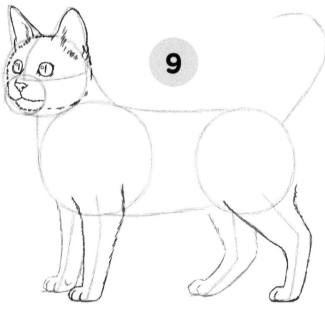

9

Draw the legs on the other side of the body using the first ones as templates.

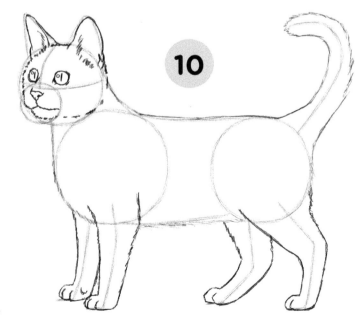

10

Use the remaining lines and shapes as guides to draw the rest of the body. Don't forget to use quick, short strokes in the furry areas.

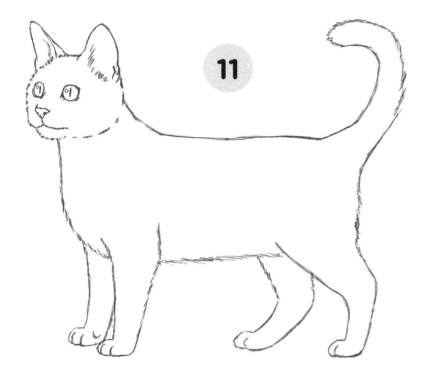

Erase guide lines and tidy up your drawing. You are now ready to add the complex Bengal pattern, so take a deep breath!

ROSETTES Leopards, ocelots, margays, and other wild cats also have rosettes. When drawing rosettes, don't make them perfect; use distorted shapes for a more organic feel. As you add value on this pattern, use strokes that go in the general direction of the fur. Add a few small spots inside some of the rosettes. The outsides of the rosettes and the spots inside should be dark, and the centers should have a medium value.

Bengals have a distinctive coat pattern made up of stripes, rosettes, and spots. Using a dark value, add stripes on the forehead and on the cheeks. Continue the stripes along the body and note where they come together to form the oval-like rosettes. Gradually turn the rosettes into thick stripes toward the tail and into spots toward the feet. Then use a medium value on the insides of the rosettes and a light value on the rest of the body. Before finishing, add few shadows to give the body more dimension and volume, and don't forget the cast shadow.

PERSIAN

1

Lightly draw two big circles on your paper as a guide for the Persian kitten's head and body. Leave enough room on the bottom for the feet and tail.

2

Add two construction lines in the head to help you place the facial features later. Then connect the head and body circles with lines. The line on the left should curve outward quite a bit to create the guide for the chest.

3

Draw a circle on the bottom half of the head as a guide for the muzzle. Then add the guides for the front legs and paws with simple lines and shapes.

4

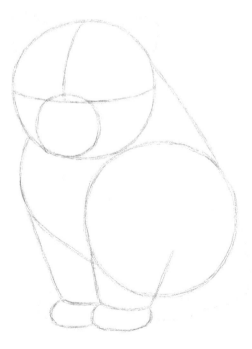

Draw two arcs or triangle shapes on top of the head. Then finish the rear end of the body that is sitting on the ground, as well as the shapes for the hind paws.

5

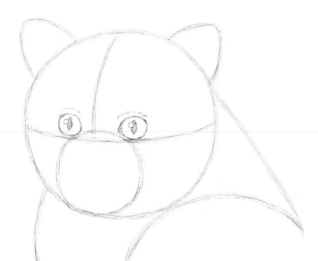

Sketch the eyes lightly so that they're easy to erase if you don't get them right at first. The eye on the right should be a tiny bit bigger and wider than the eye on the left because of perspective. Add a series of lines around the outside of the eyes for the fur.

6

Draw the upturned nose and a curved line that's made up of quick, short strokes above the nose to convey the flatness of the muzzle. Then draw the mouth and add a few dashes and dots to create the base of the whiskers.

7

Draw the ears with quick, short pencil strokes.

8

Finish the wide head with longer strokes to convey the fluffiness of the fur.

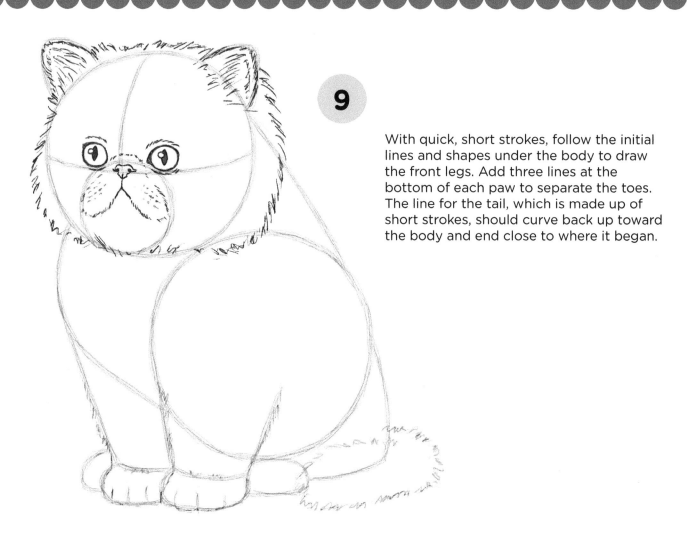

9

With quick, short strokes, follow the initial lines and shapes under the body to draw the front legs. Add three lines at the bottom of each paw to separate the toes. The line for the tail, which is made up of short strokes, should curve back up toward the body and end close to where it began.

Draw what's visible of the hind paws the same way you drew the front paws. Then use the remaining lines and shapes as guides to draw the rest of the body. Use long pencil strokes to represent the long fur, and add a few to the chest to give it a fluffier texture.

10

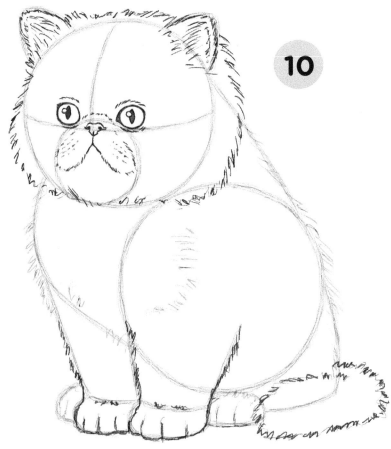

11

Erase the guide lines to tidy up your sketch.

12

Add some shadows to give your Persian more dimension and volume. Stop after that if you'd like your kitten to be white, or add even more value for extra detail. Persians can have a variety of coat patterns, so feel free to shade yours however you'd like. A rough value gives the coat a furry texture, so don't shade too smoothly. Mostly focus on adding the strokes in the basic direction that the fur should go. As you add the value, separate each individual stroke a bit so that the white of the paper comes through. That will make your pencil strokes read as fur.

CALICO

1

Lightly sketch three circles as guides for the head and body. Note how the head circle overlaps one of the body circles.

2

Add two construction lines in the head to help you place the facial features later. Connect the head and body circles with horizontal lines. Then add the guides for the front legs and paws with simple lines and shapes.

3

Finish up your guide lines in this step, adding a small circle for the muzzle, triangles for ears, and the guides for the hind legs and tail with simple shapes.

4

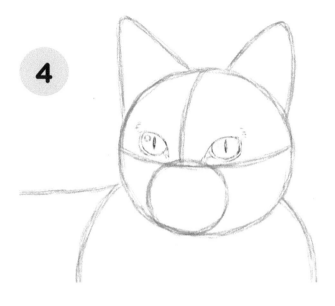

Sketch the eyes inside the head and darken your lines once you're happy with the shapes and placement. Include a few lines outside of the eyes for detail.

PUPILS You can also make the pupils bigger and rounder or extremely thin slits. Off to the side of each pupil, draw a tiny circle for a highlight. Shade the pupils, but don't overlap the inside of the highlight circles.

5

Sketch the triangular nose, and once you are happy with the shape, darken the lines. Then, using quick, short pencil strokes, add two lines above the nose for the bridge, the mouth, and the chin.

6

Finalize the shapes of the ears, and then finish up the furry head. Use a series of strokes inside the ears and along the shape of the face to create a fur-like texture. Don't forget a couple of lines in the face for detail.

Use the guides for the legs that you already drew to complete the legs and paws. Add small, curved lines to create the toes.

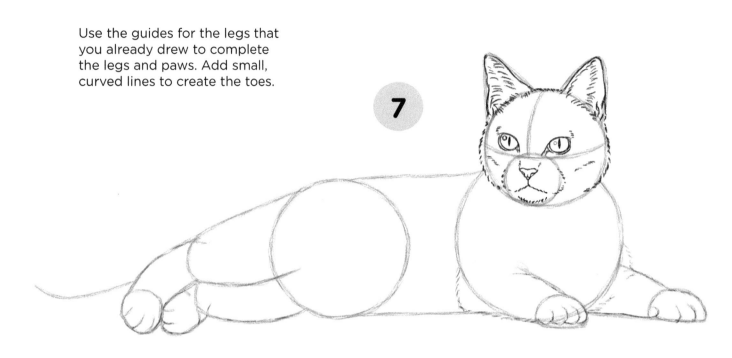

Using the remaining lines and shapes as guides to finish the body and tail. Follow the path of the guide and draw a series of strokes along it to make it look furry.

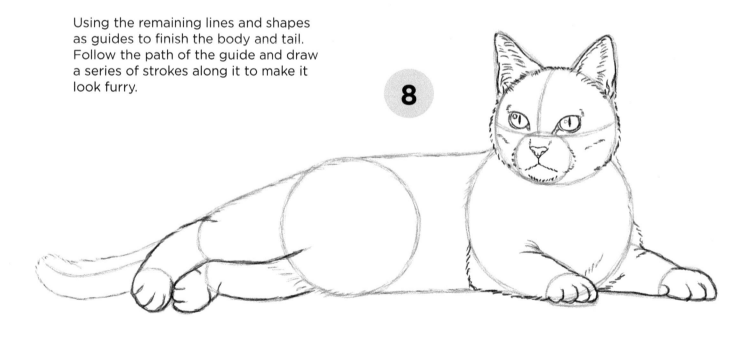

For a cleaner look, erase as much as you can of the initial guide lines, and then clean up your sketch.

9

When shading, vary the pressure on your pencil to get different degrees of tonal value. There are light values around on the face, feet, and underside of the body. The pattern contains medium and dark values. There are some shadows under the head and on the legs and stomach. Finally, add a cast shadow underneath the body so your cat doesn't appear to be floating.

10

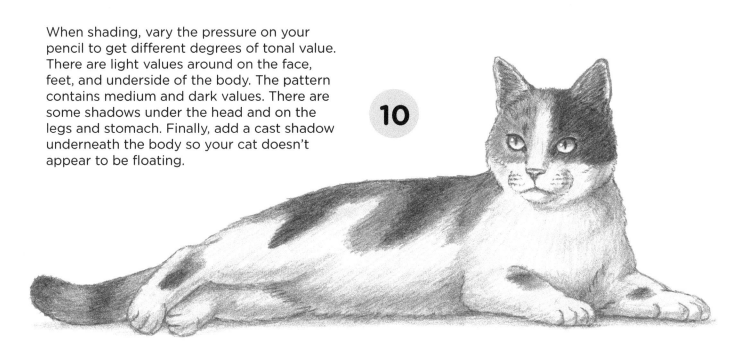

MAINE COON

1

Draw a large circle as a guide for the top part of the Maine Coon's body. Then draw a smaller circle for the head, with two curved guide lines inside of it. Then add a curved line at the bottom of the body.

2

Finish up the guide lines with the ears, muzzle, neck, legs, and tail shapes.

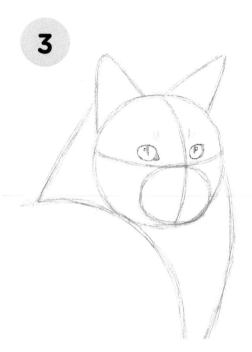

3

Draw the eyes, including the pupils and highlight circles. Then add some short strokes above the eyes for the brow.

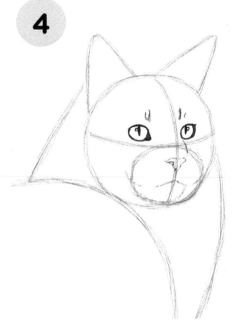

4

Draw the muzzle, including the nose, wide mouth, and wide chin under the mouth. Use quick, short strokes to represent fur.

5

Follow the path of the triangle guides as you darken the lines and create the structure of the ears. Add the tufts of hair on the tip of the ear using quick pencil strokes and add some fur inside the ear the same way.

6

Use the initial shapes and lines as guides to draw the rest of the head. Notice how long the pencil strokes are to create the furry texture.

7

Additional lines inside the head help emphasize the shape of the face under all that fur. Add the whiskers inside the muzzle using longer strokes.

8

Use the lines under the body as guides to draw the three visible legs. The tops of the legs are wider than the bottoms, and add small, curved lines for toes.

9

For the body, follow the basic path of the guides to represent the long fur. Add another line of strokes under the neck for the fluffy fur found on the chest.

10

Use the curved line at the bottom as a guide to draw the thick, fluffy tail.

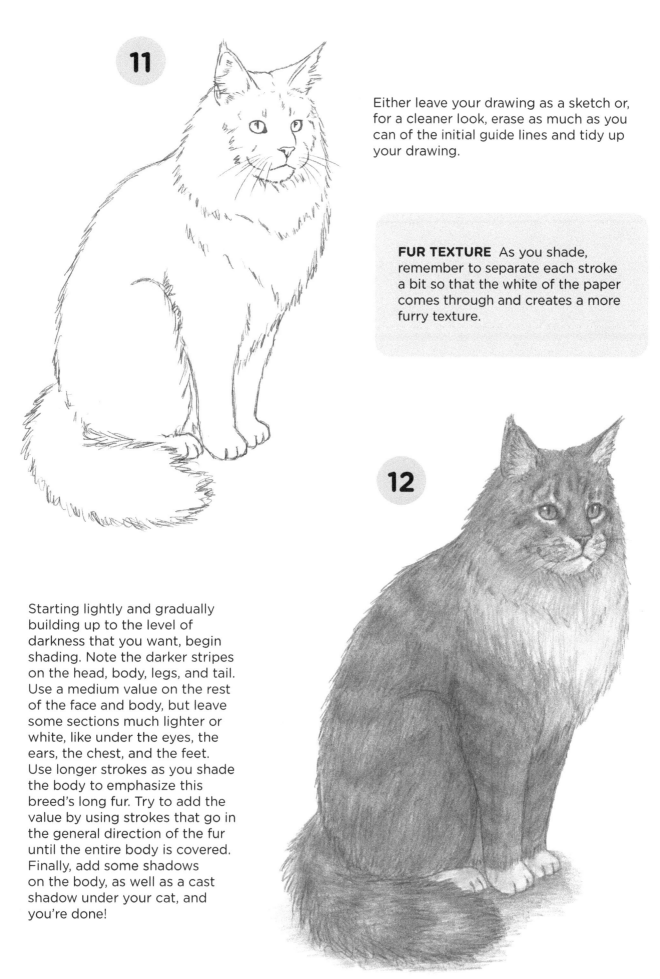

11

Either leave your drawing as a sketch or, for a cleaner look, erase as much as you can of the initial guide lines and tidy up your drawing.

FUR TEXTURE As you shade, remember to separate each stroke a bit so that the white of the paper comes through and creates a more furry texture.

12

Starting lightly and gradually building up to the level of darkness that you want, begin shading. Note the darker stripes on the head, body, legs, and tail. Use a medium value on the rest of the face and body, but leave some sections much lighter or white, like under the eyes, the ears, the chest, and the feet. Use longer strokes as you shade the body to emphasize this breed's long fur. Try to add the value by using strokes that go in the general direction of the fur until the entire body is covered. Finally, add some shadows on the body, as well as a cast shadow under your cat, and you're done!

ABOUT THE AUTHOR

How2DrawAnimals.com teaches beginning artists how to draw all kinds of animals from A to Z through video demonstrations and simple step-by-step instructions. Started in 2012 by an animal-loving artist with a bachelor's degree in illustration, How2DrawAnimals offers a new tutorial each week and now boasts hundreds of animal drawing tutorials. Working in graphite and in colored pencils, and in both realistic and cartoon styles, How2DrawAnimals has featured animals from all letters of the alphabet, from Aardvark to Zebra and everything in between. See more at How2DrawAnimals.com.

ALSO IN THE LET'S DRAW SERIES:

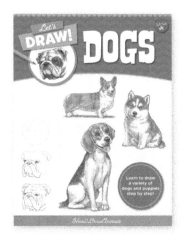

Let's Draw Dogs
ISBN: 978-0-7603-8072-7

Let's Draw Favorite Animals
ISBN: 978-0-7603-8074-1

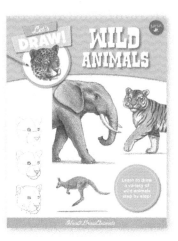

Let's Draw Wild Animals
ISBN: 978-0-7603-8076-5

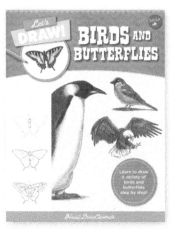

Let's Draw Birds & Butterflies
ISBN: 978-0-7603-8078-9

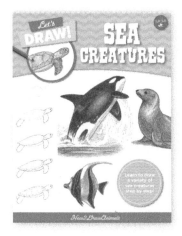

Let's Draw Sea Creatures
ISBN: 978-0-7603-8080-2

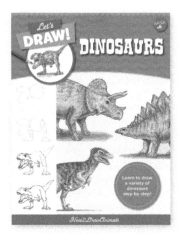

Let's Draw Dinosaurs
ISBN: 978-0-7603-8082-6

Let's Draw Dragons
ISBN: 978-0-7603-8084-0

The Quarto Group

Inspiring | Educating | Creating | Entertaining

www.WalterFoster.com

CPSIA information can be obtained
at www.ICGtesting.com
Printed in the USA
JSHW061208181122
33414JS00004B/10